DOUBLE FEAT

Sam Meets the Loch Monster
&
Facts about the Loch Ness Monster for Kids

Early Reader
Children's Picture Books

Written By: Bella Wilson & Lisa Barry

Illustrated By: Kissel Cablayda & Jonalyn Crisologo

JD-Biz Publishing

Table of Contents

Dad has some great news. He's won a holiday vacation in a competition. A two week holiday anywhere in the world! Sam claps his hands and jumps up and down.

"Where shall we go"? He asks. "To Scotland!"
Mom suggests. "My granny came from there".
So it's settled. Scotland it is.

Up in his room, Sam looks up Scotland in his atlas. It's on a small island called Great Britain, and Scotland looks very small indeed.

Scotland is famous for whisky, kilts, tartan, and Loch Ness, the deepest lake in Britain, which has a monster in it. Sam decides he'd like to see the monster for himself.

Sam has never been on a plane before, and he's a bit scared as the engines roar and the plane leaves the ground. The roads and buildings get smaller and smaller, and then they are in the clouds and on their way.

There are pretty ladies on the plane who put Sam's seatbelt on, then bring him drinks, food, and a blanket. Sam watches a movie about superheroes and falls asleep.

Sam wakes up as the plane lands. He's back in another airport that looks exactly like the one he just left! "All airports look a bit like each other" Dad says. Dads know about these kinds of things.

After driving through the big busy city of
Glasgow the roads become very small and
narrow. There are very few houses too, and
hardly any trees.

Then there are hills, hills, and more hills, covered by yellow bushes which Mom calls gorse, and more purple ones called heather. Sam laughs. "Don't be silly Mommy. Heather's a girl's name!" Mom smiles because her name is Heather.

They stop at the top of a hill to look at the
view. "That's Loch Ness. 'Loch' is the
Scottish word for 'lake'" "The one with the
monster in it"? Sam asks. Mom nods.
"WOW"! Sam thinks. "If only I could meet
the monster."

There is a strange man standing there. He's very tall, with a rugged face and bright red cheeks. He has a HUMONGOUS red beard and he's wearing a colourful checked skirt with a little pouch on it. There's also a huge black furry thing on his head.

At his feet there's a small shaggy black dog. It has short legs and pointy ears. Mom says it's a Scottish Terrier.

Dad tosses some coins in the man's cap and
the big red man lifts something onto his
shoulder. It looks like a great fat checked
pillow with pipes sticking out of it. Mom says
they're bagpipes. They make the weirdest
sound, a bit like a cat howling at night.

Next they continue driving around the Loch until they reach their hotel. Sam doesn't take his eyes off the lake in case the monster pops its head out, but nothing happens.

The hotel looks just like a castle. Inside there's another man with a skirt on. "Why do the men wear skirts?" Sam asks. Mom laughed "They're kilts. Scotsmen are very proud of them".

Sam decides to slip outside to do some exploring. Mom tells him not to go too far as it's getting dark and she doesn't want him to get lost. Sam goes down to the water's edge and looks out into the loch.

He throws a stone into the water, then another, then decides to go back to the hotel. It's a bit creepy here. He can imagine monsters in the water. He turns to go, but then -

– the water in the loch is boiling just like a pot of water on the stove, hissing and bubbling. And then - Sam can't believe his eyes!

Slowly, out of the water a great pointed head
appears, then a long, long neck and the front
bit of an enormous, scaly greenish-brown
body. Sam can see huge sharp teeth too.

Sam starts walking backward, trying not to move suddenly, in case he startles the monster, but it cocks its head to one side and says: "Don't be afraid. I won't hurt you. What's your name"?

Her voice is very deep and rumbling but her eyes are green and kind. Maybe she's not the fierce monster everyone talks about at all! He gulps. "I'm S-S-Sam" he stutters.

"Pleased to meet you, Sam". The monster says politely. She has the same Scottish voice as everyone else he's met so far. "What do you think of my loch?"

"It's lovely, Ma'am" he says, smiling a trembly smile. Nessie smiles back in a monsterish sort of way. "Don't be formal. Call me Nessie. I like boys."

Sam's heart races. He could feel it hammering in his chest. "F-for lunch"? He asks. "Are you going to eat me"?

Nessie laughs a great big, rumbling, booming laugh. "Of course not!" She said. "Just to pass the time with."

Sam is fascinated. He was standing here
actually talking to the Loch Ness monster!

Sam sits down. He's not afraid any more.
They sit and chat for a while then Sam notices
that it's getting dark. "I have to go," he says.
"Thanks for the chat." Nessie looks sad as she
watches him leave. The loch is very lonesome
sometimes.

Back at the hotel Mom and Dad run out to hug him. "Where have you been?" They ask. They look very worried. "Talking to the Loch Ness Monster," he replied. "She's very nice." "There's no such thing as the Loch Ness Monster." Dad says.

"There is. I saw her and we chatted about all sorts of things. She's really kind and not a bit scary". "What an imagination" Dad says.

Sam looks back. He sees a monsterish head disappearing under the waves then looks at the big brownish-green scale in his hand and smiles. He knows better!

Facts about the Loch Ness Monster for Kids

Fig. 1. Artistic interpretation of Nessie, the Loch Ness Monster, as a misunderstood creature.

Europe has fascinated audiences throughout history with its literature, rich with legends—stories of noble kings and brave knights battling fiery dragons. In this Modern Age, who would have known that it had one more card up its sleeve of magic and wonders?

The largest loch in Britain, Loch Ness offers splendid scenery that has enchanted the world with its puzzle.

Dinosaurs have left fossils for archaeologists to excavate. Dragons have filled the pages of folklore and served as fine pieces of art. And the mysterious loch has Nessie, the Loch Ness Monster. However, unlike dinosaurs, dragons, and other ancient mythical figures, Nessie has carefully kept her tracks covered—almost!

The unfolding tale of Nessie began in 565 AD. It is believed that an Irish monk, Saint Columba, happened to be at the loch when a native was killed by the beast. He ordered his follower to dive into the water. The moment the formidable creature surfaced, he banished the brute away by signing the cross and uttering these words: "Go no further. Do not touch the man. Go back at once."

During the 1930's, more people reported Nessie sightings after the road construction by the loch. Among the claimants, a motorcyclist and a couple driving by, narrated how the legendary creature came out of the woods and crossed the street back to the loch. When asked, they said the "monster" merely spared them a glance and went on its way.

Others turned in photos and sonar readings as proof. And this year, Apple took the world aback when it claimed it had finally captured Nessie! Only… through satellite, that is.

Is Nessie truly a fearsome monster haunting the waters of the Scottish loch? Could she simply be a myth invented by mischievous minds for the purpose of creating havoc or attracting tourists? Or is she a misunderstood mammal keeping her peace, remaining hidden by the safety of the deep?

In this delightful book, Lisa Barry explores the recorded accounts about Nessie. Lisa takes no leaning and provides an unbiased, straightforward discourse, rousing the reader's curious mind. It is as thought-provoking as Nessie herself.

This makes a wonderful addition to the family and library collection.

Fig. 2. There exists hardly any ancient text of Nessie's existence—exempting the "Life of Saint Columba" by Adomnán, a 7th century writer. According to the book, Saint Columba single-handedly kept the beast from devouring a man in 565 AD.

Facts about the Loch

The word loch finds its origin in the Gaelic language of the Irish and Scots. It means lake or sea inlet. The Loch Ness is located in northern Scotland and it is fresh water, which means it does not have salty sea water in it. This particular loch is enormous; in fact it is the biggest in Britain. It is enormous enough to outdo all other British lochs and lakes combined!

The Loch Ness is roughly twenty-two and a half miles long, and around one and a half miles wide. Apparently, it has a depth of 754 feet. However, some say there is evidence that suggests part of the loch goes as deep as 812 feet. It holds 263 thousand million cubic feet of water. It has a surface area of 14,000 acres. If all the water was emptied from the loch, it could fit 10 times the world's population.

The loch was formed around 500 million years ago. Scientists say that tremors caused the earth to crack open, creating a space that became the loch. The Ice Age, which occurred about 12,000 years ago, left the planet covered in ice. Needless to say, the loch was no exception. The hard ice formed the landscape with the harsh and steep inclines to the loch, which we see today.

In the depths of the loch is a fault line, which caused the tremors millions of years ago. However, it still affects the area to this day. The last tremor was recorded in 1997. Statistics also show that the mountains around within its perimeters are rising at an approximated rate of 1mm per year. Certain skeptics think that this caused of some of the supposed Nessie sightings. They explain that the fault line causes water disturbances, which affect the surface in unusual ways.

The underground fault line also keeps Loch Ness from freezing. Even though the temperature rises to a chilling level on the surface of the water (the Scottish air is very cold indeed), it remains quite warm close to the bottom. At times, the fusion of the warm and cold water creates steam. This meshes well with the creepy environment of the loch, intensifying its eerie ambiance.

That is just for starters. Apparently, Loch Ness is radioactive! In 1986 a nuclear power plant in Chernobyl, located in the former Soviet Union, exploded. A radioactive cloud caused by the blast, travelled across Europe. Scientists have found radioactive sediment in the loch, resulting from the Chernobyl disaster. This resulted in the Loch Ness' radioactivity!

Facts about the Loch Ness Monster

The first account of a monster seen in Loch Ness was written by Adomnán, a 7th century writer. According to his book, *Life of Saint Columba*, it was in 565 AD when Saint Columba, an Irish monk traveling through Scotland in missionary work, encountered a group of Picts. They were carrying the corpse of a man, who was supposedly attacked by a "water beast." In that instant, Saint Columba sent his follower, named Luigne Moccu Min, to swim across the lake. When the beast appeared, he sent it away by signing the cross and uttering the words: "Go no further. Do not touch the man. Go back at once."

No other ancient or historical records have been established to support this. It is necessary for the inquisitive minds to remember that there were many rumored sea monsters all over Europe. The continent's literature is filled with tales of terrible reptilian-like beings. Many ancient creatures also received "bad press." Either rumors of their potent healing powers or threat to humanity caused many of these beasts to be hunted and slaughtered.

For instance, people of the Medieval Age were quite engrossed and convinced of the existence of unicorns. Many believed that they were driven to extinction because they were believed of possessing healing wonders that were derived from its horn. This prompted many elite into hunting sprees. The life of the supposed mythic creatures was the price for such potent elixir.

There are other explanations to the existence of reptilian-like creatures, associating them to dragons, serpents, or *Draconians* (prevalent figures, which have been revered and feared). Depending on which chronicles you come upon, they may be malevolent or benevolent beings. There are many opposing texts, requiring discernment from the earnest and resolute seeker.

Here is another historical aspect to consider. The year 565 AD falls under the Medieval Era—a time of socio-political unrest that affected the religious front. The Roman Catholic Church was no exemption. Political and religious propagandas were prevalent to expand, fortify, and enforce the authority of those in power.

Similarly, the fabrication of tales proved to be an excellent tool even in the household. Mothers and nannies are especially fond of using this method, to cause fear and get little naughty children to comply and follow their bidding. Most parents will reason that it is necessary to instill discipline.

However, this should, in no way, be sought as a conclusion to undermine the possibilities that there, indeed, was an encounter between the monk and the beast at the loch. By keeping our minds open to all the possibilities, it would be of our benefit to consider the countless data that eventually poured in during modern times. An open mind is necessary to reach a truthful and impartial conclusion.

Moreover, by keeping our minds open and combining it with better judgment, we must remember that ancient knowledge transformed into fables—or altered. Many were also completely destroyed or kept secret for a variety of reasons, mostly of which to keep the populace from gaining access to ancient knowledge. This is why a critical mind is especially important, when analyzing all information presented.

It was not until the 1900's when more sightings were reported. The completion of the road by the loch lured more people into the area, thereby inviting attention to it as well.

The Nessie fever hit an all-time high in 1933. A newspaper publication contributed to the areas publicity, attracting the attention of people. Many travelers were passing by the area regularly. And sightings increased.

Eventually, the monster was given the affectionate nickname "Nessie." This name means "pure" in the Scottish language. Many people began to conjure up images and analyze the little evidences of her existence, because no one has actually chanced upon Nessie. One hypothesis that came about assumes that she is a sea serpent that got stuck in the loch many years ago.

Others believe the Loch Ness Monster is a type of dinosaur called a plesiosaur. This type of dinosaur lived in water. They are closely related to lizards, which strongly resembles the plesiosaur's body structure and long neck. They could swim faster than the fastest swimmer in the world. Plesiosaurs have been extinct for 65 million years. This is precisely the reason our friend from Loch Ness immediately piqued the interest and curiosity of scientists. One of the problems with the dinosaur theory is that plesiosaur's had lungs. This means they had to come up from the water to breath. If this was the case with Nessie, some deduce that there would be a more sightings and, perhaps, credible evidences.

According to reports, she has been spotted in the water and on the land around the loch. This could mean Nessie is an amphibian, an animal that can breathe under water and outside of it. Frogs and toads are also amphibians.

Some witnesses describe Nessie as a creature with a head that looks like a snake, two or four flippers, two humps, and a tail. The largest of her humps is estimated to be 50 feet long. This is one of the images that have been put together based on the evidence collected over the years.

Others completely disagree. They say she has small horns; others say that she is hairy! The different ideas about Nessie make her interesting. To top it all off, no actual body parts or live monster has been found and studied! Thus, everyone has different opinions.

The local legends about a beast in the loch go back even further than the first official sighting. Local people used to tell their children a scary story. They would say that when the monsters of the lake were hungry they would transform into horses. If someone got on one of these horse creatures, they would be kidnapped. The "horse" would ride into the Loch and turn back into the monster before eating the poor victim. They called these creatures "Kelpies". Legends like these are found around the world, not just in Loch Ness.

People are all very used to hearing about Nessie, the one creature lurking under the deep waters of the Loch. However, if she is under there, she most certainly has a family, and a big one at that. For a creature of any kind to survive in the loch for all these years, there would have to be several of them, considering that they have reproduced.

Some merely dismiss Nessie as a myth—a figment of people's wild imagination and that she does not exist at all. Skeptics surmise that the monster tale was made up to lure in travelers, and boost local tourism and sales.

Other critics conclude that witnesses may have mistaken waves, logs, and other sea animals (such as seals or the manatee) for the monster.

Nevertheless, many feel strongly about the existence of the Loch Ness Monster, either way. People have debated the authenticity of her existence, and will probably continue to do so for years to come.

One thing is certain: Nessie has made Scotland and the Loch Ness famous around the world! According to a survey conducted in 2006, the Loch Ness Monster is the most prominent Scottish figure. She beat the well-known actor, former James Bond, Sean Connery. That is quite an achievement for a monster that may not even exist!

Nessie Sightings

Over the years, many claimed to have spotted the monster of Loch Ness, although Nessie does not seem to like her photo being taken very much. Thus, these sightings have provided few evidences. It is up to readers to render their verdict.

Fig. 3. Since the road construction by the loch, more Nessie sightings have been reported. In 1933, a couple claimed the creature came out of the woods and crossed the road just as they were driving by the loch.

Some sightings may have been an honest mistake, such that the people may have confused a log or seal for the monster. However, there are those who take the time to make things up just for fun. Others are just looking for attention or attempting to boost tourism in the area.

Below are accounts of reported instances, when Nessie had been spotted. Look at what they have to say. Do you believe them?

Nessie Spotted on Land

1879 - A group of children saw an elephant-like creature walk into the water.

1880 - Two men spotted a large grey creature with a long neck walk from the woods into the water.

1912 - Five children say they saw a sandy colored creature that looked like a small camel walk into the water.

1923 - A man claimed he saw a green animal with a 12 foot body and a tail the same length. It had four legs, with feet that looked like that of an elephant.

1930 - A group of children saw a "peculiar and horrifying animal" in the bushes.

1933 - A woman saw a 25 foot grey creature with humps. Its feet were like a pig but bigger.

1933 - A woman saw a large "hairy hippo".

1934 - A woman saw a big dark creature with a small head and long tail moving fast towards the water.

1960 - A man spotted a 45 foot dark creature with flippers and paddles. The tail looked like an elephant's trunk.

Nessie Spotted in the Water

1871 - A man noticed a slow moving log that suddenly moved very fast.

1885 - A man exclaimed, "Biggest thing I ever saw in my life!" He claimed that the creature had a horse's head with a mane.

1895 - Fishermen and hotel owners reported a Nessie sighting. The official quote from these spotters was, "Horrible great beastie!"

1908 - A man claimed he saw a 30- to 40-foot creature. It was still in the water.

1929 - A married couple described the creature as a one having a hump that was as big as a horse.

1933 - A man saw the creature's head laying low in the water catching fish with its mouth open. Mouth width was estimated to be 12 to 18 inches.

1933 - A married couple observed a 25 feet by two feet creature, which caused lots of splashing. There was a single hump visible.

1933 - A man saw two humps in the water. He estimated the creature was 20 feet. It was very fast. It submerged under water immediately when a car horn sounded.

1934 - A man saw a creature that was swimming on its side. He estimated it was 24 feet long. He saw three humps. He also claimed it had a mane.

1954 - A family of four claimed the 30-foot long creature had one hump and moved slowly.

1956 - A big group of people at a party saw a single hump, measuring about 4 feet.

1960 - A man thought he saw a creature, measuring eight feet long with a two feet hump.

1960 - A married couple, together with a whole small yacht crew, spotted a 10-foot hump.

1960 - Vicar and his wife. This man from the church and his wife saw two humps emerging out of the loch.

1963 - A married couple saw four humps coming out of the water.

1964 - A married couple reported seeing a straight pole like creature which moved quickly when the car door slammed.

1966 - A married couple saw a creature, measuring 30 feet long with three humps.

1969 - Two men spotted two humps. They said it could be seen moving really fast. These men estimated it was a total of 24 feet in length.

1973 - A man says he just saw a pole-like creature.

1979 - A man noticed a black object. He said it could be seen moving fast in the water.

1996 - A man observed a single hump rising from the water.

1996 - Hotel staff noticed black humps in the loch. It was seen by all of the hotel staff.

1998 - Four people saw a large object with a long tail in the water.

2011 - A man spotted a black hump rising from the water.

Sonar Evidence

People often use sonar equipment to search for Nessie. This is because the loch is very large and deep. Using sonar enables them to search large spaces that cannot be physically reached. Sonar is the same technique animals, such as whales and dolphins, use to communicate. When noises are made, noise waves are transmitted. These will hit objects that come along the path of noise waves, reflecting back to the origin. This mechanics behind this is similar to hearing an echo. It is the noise reflected back to you.

George Edwards is a Nessie hunter. He spends a great deal of time looking for the Loch Ness Monster. He uses sonar for his searches. During one of his explorations, he found indications that part of the loch drops from 754 to 812 feet. This is significant, because it was previously believed that the bottom of the loch was as flat as a football field. This new finding revealed that there is still more to learn about the loch. Moreover, those deep trenches may lead to a network of caves, where Nessie and her family probably dwell. Hence, the newly discovered cavernous space had been aptly dubbed "Nessie's Lair." Others call it as "Edwards Deep," in reference to George Edwards.

Others who have tried to capture Nessie through sonar have reported strange shapes visible in the area. The first reported "sonar sighting" was long ago in 1968. This had been supplemented by nine more official reports, turning in findings of strange, unexplainable large shapes deep in the water. Unfortunately, the sonar does not give us a picture like a photograph. Sonar experts are required to read and interpret the results.

Fig.4. In 2014, the tech company, Apple, stunned its competitors and reignited the interest of Nessie hunters, when it released a satellite data showing a massive figure in the Loch Ness. The form undoubtedly resembled descriptions reported through the years. However, the satellite image still remains in question, due to the lack of a clear, face-to-face encounter with Nessie.

Searches for Nessie

The Circus Search

At the beginning at the 1900's the excitement surrounding the possible existence of Nessie grew. With this, so did the number of reports. In 1933, a circus owner named Bertrum Mills offered £20.000 to anyone who was able to bring Nessie alive to his circus. This was a huge amount during that time. It drew people to flock in Loch Ness, in the hopes of claiming the prize. Fortunately for Nessie, none of them were successful.

Sir Edward Mountain Search

In 1934, Sir Edward Mountain launched a search, funding a considerable amount of people and equipment. The result? Apparently, Sir Edward and his crew sighted the monster! They had taken a number of photographs. However, these no longer serve as substantial proof in our modern age. Considering our technological advancement, the antiquated quality of the photos does not meet the expectation of our times.

Operation Deepscan

In 1987, Operation Deepscan was the biggest sonar exploration of the loch ever undertaken. Television and newspaper crews from around the world gathered to the loch to cover the event, expecting to see a monster. On the first day, the operation reported back three unexplainable sonar readings. They were described as in-between the size of a shark and a whale. It was not as huge as what some eye witnesses claimed of Nessie, but the length was big enough to perplex experts. A size that large could not be any known fish or animal residing in the loch.

The following day returned no unusual sonar readings, or anything of importance for that matter. The media lost interest, and the whole project had gone down in history as a failure. People expected something thrilling and dramatic, such as a monster being pulled from the dark murky waters. When they realized it was not going to happen, they got bored and left.

This frustrated Nessie-believers. They considered Deepscan a success by finding those three unusual sonar readings on the first day. They may have a valid argument, because the operation surveyed on 60% of the loch.

Project Urquhart

This project was named after the Urquhart castle, of which vestiges still remain standing by the loch. It was Nicholas Witchell, a BBC TV presenter who organized the project. He had been a lover of Loch Ness and the possibility of a monster for a long time. In 1992, he finally decided to deploy a big search party, composed of scientific experts.

The operation was sponsored by major television networks and organizations, including Discovery Channel, BBC, and The Natural History Museum. However, the sponsors refused to be officially identified with the search because the Loch Ness Monster had been highly considered a fake during the 1990's. They did not want to risk appearing ridiculous for shelling out a fortune in search for a mythic creature. This sufficed. Simply funding the exploit offered a great opportunity for further study.

The team was equipped with the latest sonar technology of the time. It enabled them to take seven million sonar pictures. They discovered a new depth of 786 feet. The evidence in this study pointed to a flat surface at the bottom, similar to a football field. This contradicted the previous findings by George Edwards.

The results also returned images that appeared to be a series of footprints underwater. Closer investigation revealed that the prints were manmade, most likely created when the army was testing sonar technology many years ago.

Just like previous studies in the loch, the sonar readings also indicated a very unusual shape. They managed to follow this shape for two minutes. It also generated an echo that was stronger and bigger than any of the identified fishes residing in the loch.

The study continued for a couple of years. In 1993, they proceeded with studying the fish and plant life within the loch. The results have not been properly explained. They found fish in parts of the loch they did not expect to, and little or no fish where they expected more. The same applied for every aspect of life in the loch. Again, this demonstrated that Loch Ness is still shrouded with mystery, most of which cannot be explained by skeptics.

The same year, the National History Museum began its own investigations. It was their job to look at microscopic creatures (living things too small to be seen with our eyes, and require special equipment to be observed) in the loch. They found a new microscopic worm, which was previously unknown to science. They also struggled to find the specific types of microscopic worms, which scientists expected to find in the loch.

As for Nessie, further sonar exploration brought in more strange readings. Similar to previous readings, they were too big to be fishes in the loch. However, there had been no conclusive data published establishing Nessie's existence.

Nessie Hoaxes

Since the 1930's, people have been pretending to find evidence of the Loch Ness monster for varying reasons. Whatever their reasons, these tricksters annoy the true believers more than anyone else. After years of hoaxes, the general public has grown very skeptical whenever new sightings come to light. People refuse to be the center of ridicule. Thus, some believe witnesses have become reluctant to submit reports.

Here is a list of some famous Nessie hoaxes:

In 1933, a foot was found that was claimed to be from the monster. It was soon discovered that it belonged to a hippopotamus. This was the first of many official hoaxes.

In 1934, a photograph was taken, revealing the head of a creature that looks like a dinosaur. This has been called "the surgeon's photo" because the man who took it was a doctor. It was not until he was on his death bed that he admitted it was a hoax, and the dinosaur-shaped head had been placed on a toy submarine.

In 1951, a man took a photograph of three humps. He later admitted it was a hoax, after receiving massive public criticism. He said he covered three bales of hay with tarpaulin, and placed them in the loch to fake the photo.

On April 1, 1972, a body of the Loch Ness monster was found. This turned out to be an April fool's joke and was, in fact, the body of an elephant seal from the Atlantic.

A man who hunted for Nessie for 10 years admitted that many of his pictures were cut-and-pasted pictures of dinosaurs. This was prior to the digital age. Thus, he literally cut and pasted these photographs.

In 1975, a man named Peter Scott took a picture, which he claimed to show a flipper. Believing it would suffice as evidence, he officially named the creature "Nessiteras Rhombopteryx." He said this meant "The Ness wonder with a diamond fin". However, if you look closer at the name and re-arrange the letters, a new phrase is discovered: "monster hoax by Sir Peter S." However, Peter denies that this was on purpose.

In 2001, someone placed Conger Eels by the side of the loch. It was discovered that these were not related to Nessie because the eels live in salt water—the loch consists of fresh water.

In 2003, a fossil was found by the loch. It clearly showed part of a plesiosaur. When scientists studied it though, they discovered that the fossil was made of limestone that was not part from the loch. They concluded that the "fossil" was purposefully placed by someone.

In 2005, a big tooth was found. Apparently, it was discovered in the side of a deer by the loch. The tooth went "missing," but experts recognized it from the picture as an antler from a deer.

Fact or Fiction? You decide!

There are many different theories about what Nessie is. Experts have opposing views regarding the theories. Now, it is your turn to decide. Is Nessie fact or fiction?

1. **Theory:** Nessie is a plesiosaur dinosaur.

   Argument Supporting: The sightings depict a creature that looks like a plesiosaur. Plesiosaurs' have lungs. This means they need to surface from time to time for air, just like whales.

   Argument Against: If Nessie is a plesiosaur, there ought to be more sightings.

   Your Conclusion: Fact | Fiction | Not Sure

2. **Theory:** Nessie is an amphibian-like frog.

   Argument Supporting: Similar to amphibians, Nessie seems to be able to breath in and out of water. A creature like a giant long tail newt could be the explanation.

   Argument Against: No known long tail newt is as big as people claim Nessie to be.

   Your Conclusion: Fact | Fiction | Not Sure

3. **Theory:** Nessie has a big family.

   Argument Supporting: If Nessie is real and had been around all this time, there must be several others of her kind. They would have bred and reproduced. Moreover, the amount of fish in the loch is still unknown.

Argument Against: There is not enough fish to support one monster—never mind a whole family.

Your Conclusion: Fact | Fiction | Not Sure

The Loch Ness Monster Today

The Legend of Loch Ness is famous worldwide. It has drawn a lot of attention to the little Scottish town. Without Nessie, people would have never heard of Loch Ness. Indeed, the monster has strengthened trade and tourism in the area.

There are still monster sightings to this day. In November 2011, the latest photo was taken by a couple on their holiday. People will continue to come to the area, looking for Nessie. Whether out of curiosity or to conduct a large-scale research, the mystery of the deep is still very exciting and attractive.

Among the countless investigations conducted in the area, Project Urquhart could have yielded promising results. It is considerably the longest-running and extensive exploration carried out. In spite of the fact that it has not turned in solid findings to establish Nessie's credibility, it generated invaluable information regarding the area. It invalidated "previous, unfounded assumptions" regarding the plant and animal life, as well as the loch's ecosystem as a whole.

Indeed, the loch itself holds many mysteries. After decades of investigations, scientists have not unraveled the loch's mysteries. From fish behavior and statistics to the unusual microscopic creatures, Loch Ness holds more questions than answers.

Experts and their theories provide different analyses on the matter. The truth is no one has uncovered any factual, straightforward answers. The loch stretches for miles, and runs deep. The largest explorations have never managed to cover the whole area all at once.

The earth is made up of 139 million square miles of water. Scientists believe that there are still about 230,000 creatures living in these waters, which remain undiscovered.

Is it possible that one of these undiscovered creatures could be the Loch Ness monster? What do you think?

Authors Bios

Lisa Barry was born Lisa Thomas in 1982, she grew up in Gloucester, England and moved to Wales at the age of 19 to become a primary school teacher. It was here she met her future husband. Lisa has had a varied career working with children and young people aged from 3 to 19 years old. It was only after her second child was born though that she discovered a real love of writing. With her children for inspiration she is now embarking on an exciting and rewarding new career proving that life is always full of surprises.

Bella Wilson

I was born in Scotland a long, long time ago! My parents said that from an early age (two years old) I showed artistic promise after I drew my first little face on a Cornflakes packet. After a fairly boring but happy childhood I went on to study art and teaching, whereby I got the fancy letters after my name. I came to South Africa on holiday, met my husband, fell in love, got married and had four sons. I'm currently teaching art privately. My other passion is writing and reading voraciously; nobody would recognize me without a book! My favorite things are my grandson Treyton, my cat Rascal, knitting, crochet, DRAWING - big time!, and growing my own vegetables. I believe that a random act of kindness every day can change the world, and that we are all creative in various ways, and we should celebrate it.

Illustrators Bios

Jonalyn Crisologo

Writer and Visual Artist Jonalyn Crisologo completed her degree in Bachelor of Arts in Communication at the Saint Louis University. In the past ten years, she has been writing for print and Web publishing. As an artist, she has a penchant for conventional art. In spite of this, she considers digital tools quite handy. An avid reader, she is fond of graphic novels and pop-up books. Stan Lee, Walter Moers, Maurice Sendak, and Brothers Grimm are just a few of her favorite illustrators.

Kissel Cablayda is a full time graphic artist and painter based in Davao City, Philippines. When she was 9, she won from a school editorial cartooning contest and from that day on she knew her world will revolve in arts and design. Eleven years later, she graduated with a degree in Bachelor of Arts in Communication Arts Major in Media Arts from the University of the Philippines Mindanao.

Her first and second job was terrible. So she decided to have a home based job and find her passion. Now she happily works as an online book illustrator at Mendon Cottage Books.

She believes that creativity is a journey, not a destination, and that design is an essential part of every human communication and experience. She also believes that unicorns are real.

When she is not designing, she spends her time travelling, watching TV series, reading a bunch of books and cleaning her room. She likes novels written by Chaim Potok, Sidney Sheldon and Harper Lee. She loves Filipino meat cuisine and hates vegetables.

She aspires to excel in her career and make other people's lives be less hard through art and design.

To know more about her, email her at
kisselcablayda2013@gmail.com

Our books are available at

1. Amazon.com

2. Barnes and Noble

3. Itunes

4. Kobo

5. Smashwords

6. Google Play Books

Download Free Books!
http://MendonCottageBooks.com

Publisher

JD-Biz Corp

P O Box 374

Mendon, Utah 84325

http://www.jd-biz.com/

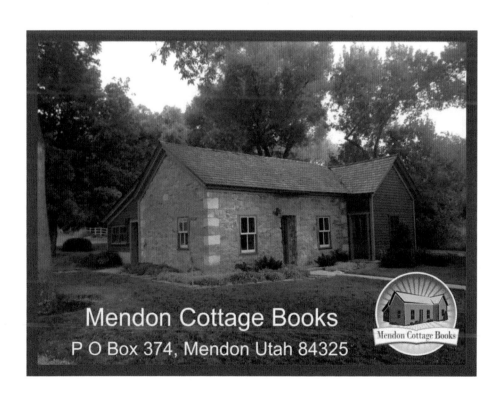

Printed in Great Britain
by Amazon

44201217R00043